CONTENTS

ABOUT THIS SERIES

History of America is a series of nine books arranged chronologically, meaning that events are described in the order in which they happened. However, each book focuses on an important person in American history, so the timespans of the titles overlap. In each book, most articles deal with a particular event or part of American history. Others deal with aspects of everyday life, such as trade, houses, clothing and farming. These general articles cover longer periods of time. The little illustrations at the top left of each article are a symbol of the times. They are identified on page 3.

▼ About the map

This map shows the United States today. It shows the boundaries and names of all the states. Refer to this map, or to the one on pages 42–43, to locate places talked about in this book.

About this book

This book is about America from 1815 to 1869. The term America means 'the United States of America', also called the USA. Much of this book tells about the Civil War. Some people call this war 'the War Between the States'. During the war, southern states were called 'slave states' and 'the Confederacy', and 'the Confederate States of America'. Northern states were called 'the Union', 'federal' and 'free states'. Words in **bold** are described in more detail in the Glossary on page 46.

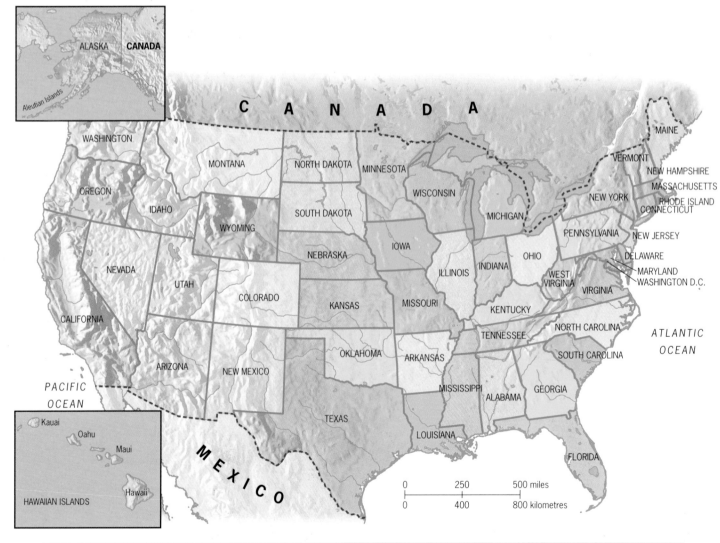

History of America
The Civil War
1815 to 1869

Sally Senzell Isaacs

First published in Great Britain by Heinemann Library,
Halley Court, Jordan Hill, Oxford OX2 8EJ,
a division of Reed Educational and Professional Publishing Ltd.
Heinemann is a registered trademark of Reed Educational & Professional
Publishing Limited.

OXFORD MELBOURNE AUCKLAND
JOHANNESBURG BLANTYRE GABORONE
IBADAN PORTSMOUTH NH (USA) CHICAGO

© Bender Richardson White 1999
© Illustrations: Bender Richardson White 1999
The moral right of the proprietor has been asserted.

HISTORY OF AMERICA: THE CIVIL WAR
was produced for Heinemann Library by Bender Richardson White.

Editor: Lionel Bender
Designer: Ben White
Assistant Editor: Michael March
Picture Researcher: Pembroke Herbert and Nancy Carter
Media Conversion and Typesetting: MW Graphics
Production Controller: Kim Richardson

03 02 01 00
10 9 8 7 6 5 4 3 2 1

500 587555

Printed in Hong Kong

British Library Cataloguing-in-Publication Data.
Isaacs, Sally Senzell
  The Civil War, 1815–69. – (History of America)
  1. United States - History - 1861–1865 - Juvenile literature
  2. United States - History - 1815–1861 - Juvenile literature
  I. Title.
  973.7

ISBN 0431 056226 Hb   ISBN 0431 05634 X Pb

Acknowledgements
The producers of this book would like to thank the following for permission to
reproduce photographs:
Picture Research Consultants, Mass: pages 6 (Illinois State Historical Library), 10
(Texas State Library & Archives Commission), 12 (Courtesy of Library of Ireland),
13 (Private Collection), 14 (Library of Congress), 16 (Library of Congress), 20l
and 20r (Library of Congress), 24 (Private Collection), 27 (Library of Congress),
29, 31 (Library of Congress), 32 (Photo Assist, Inc.), 33 (Appomattox Court
House National Historical Park), 34 (U.S. Signal Corps–Brady Collection–in the
National Archives), 36 (Library of Congress), 37 (Library of Congress), 38
(Library of Congress), 40 (Lightfoot Collection). Peter Newark's American
Pictures: pages 7, 9l, 11, 19b, 23, 26, 28, 35. North Wind Pictures: pages 19t,
25, 30, 39, 41. Corbis UK Ltd.: 9r.

Illustrations by: John James on pages 6/7, 12/13, 14/15, 16/17, 18/19,
20/21, 24/25, 28/29, 34/35, 28/29; James Field on pages 10/11, 30/31,
40/41; Mark Bergin on pages 32/33, 36/37; Gerald Wood on pages 8/9,
22/23, 26/27. All maps by Stefan Chabluk.

Cover design and make-up by Pelican Graphics. Cover artwork by John James.
Cover photos reproduced with the permission of: Top: Peter Newark's American
Pictures. Centre: Picture Research Consultants (Library of Congress). Bottom:
Peter Newark's American Pictures.

Every effort has been made to contact copyright holders of any material
reproduced in this book. Omissions will be rectified in subsequent printings if
notice is given to the publisher.

Special thanks to Mike Carpenter, Scott Westerfield and Tristan Boyer at
Heinemann Library for editorial and design guidance and direction.

For more information about Heinemann Library books, or to order, please phone
01865 888066, or send a fax to 01865 314091. You can visit our web site at
www.heinemann.co.uk

Any words appearing in the text in bold, **like this**, are
explained in the Glossary.

Major quotations used in this book come from the
following sources. Some of the quotations have been
abridged for clarity.

Page 8: Lincoln's quote about slavery from *Lincoln in His
Own Words* edited by Milton Meltzer. San Diego: Harcourt
Brace & Company, 1993, page 6.
Page 10: Lincoln's campaign speech from *Encyclopedia
of Presidents: Abraham Lincoln* by Jim Hargrove.
Chicago: Children's Press, 1988, page 33.
Page 16: Letter from Frederick Douglas from *Get On
Board: The Story of the Underground Railroad* by James
Haskins. New York: Scholastic Inc., 1993, page 27.
Page 19: President Buchanan's message from
Encyclopedia of Presidents: Abraham Lincoln by Jim
Hargrove. Chicago: Children's Press, 1988, page 70.
Page 22: Congressman's report from *The American
Nation* by James West Davidson and John E. Batchelor.
New Jersey: Prentice Hall, 1994, page 398.
Page 27: Quote by Vicksburg citizen from *The Civil War* by
Geoffrey C. Ward. New York: Alfred A. Knopf, Inc., 1990,
page 238.
Page 27: Lincoln's quote from *The Civil War "A House
Divided."* by Zachary Kent. Hillsdale, New Jersey: Enslow
Publishers, Inc., 1994, page 37.
Page 32: Sherman's quote from *The Civil War "A House
Divided"* by Zachary Kent. Hillsdale, New Jersey: Enslow
Publishers, Inc., 1994, page 87.
Page 33: Grant's quote from *The American Nation* by
James West Davidson and John E. Batchelor. New Jersey:
Prentice Hall, 1994, page 413.

The Consultants
Special thanks to Diane Smolinski, Nancy Cope
and Christopher Gibb for their help in the
preparation of this book.

INTRODUCTION

America was still a young nation around 1815. Cities were growing in the East. Towns were sprouting in new western states such as Illinois, Indiana, Kentucky and Tennessee. The next 45 years brought tremendous change. Pioneers crossed the continent to settle in western places such as Utah, Oregon, Texas and California. Railways and telegraphs began to prove that every city and town in a large nation could be connected through transportation and technology.

Much of this book describes a time when the states of America actually split into two groups. This spanned the years between 1861 and 1865. It started with arguments between people in the North and the South. They argued about how much power the **federal** government should have over the states. They argued about whether **slavery** was right or wrong. By 1861, the South formed its own government and the Civil War began. It may have been America's most tragic time.

Abraham Lincoln was president of the United States during the most crucial periods of these troubled years. More than anything else, he wanted to reunite the states. Many of the events in the book took place during Lincoln's life. Other events happened after he died. On pages that describe events during Lincoln's life, there are yellow boxes that tell you what he was doing at the time.

YOUNG ABRAHAM LINCOLN

Abraham Lincoln
Born: 12 February 1809
Father: Thomas Lincoln
Mother: Nancy Hanks
Older Sister: Sarah Lincoln.
  In 1809, the United States population was 7.2 million people, including about 1.2 million slaves.
  When Abraham was 9 years old, his mother died of a disease called milk sickness.
His father got remarried, to Sarah Bush, in 1819. She brought her three children, John, Sarah, and Matilda, into the Lincoln family.

In 1815, the United States was 39 years old. James Madison was its fourth president. The country did not yet spread from coast to coast. It did not yet include western lands, such as California, Oregon and Texas. Florida still belonged to Spain. Abraham Lincoln was six years old.

Abraham Lincoln was born near Hodgenville, Kentucky, on 12 February 1809. Kentucky, Indiana and Illinois were considered America's **frontier**. This was wilderness land just at the edge of the settled part of the nation. People moved to the frontier so that they could own more farmland. They had to clear the land, plant crops and build cabins. Even small children helped at work.

In 1816, just before Abraham – Abe, for short – turned eight, the Lincoln family moved to Indiana. Land was easier to buy there. Also, Indiana did not allow people to own **slaves**. Therefore, it was easier for newcomers, such as Abe's father, to find a job and live peaceably.

▼ In Indiana, young Abe Lincoln spent much of his time chopping trees. He cleared land for farming, cut firewood and split logs to make fences.

▶ Many historians believe that Abraham Lincoln was born in this cabin. Abraham was named after his grandfather Abraham Lincoln, who lived in the Virginia Colony and fought in the War of Independence of 1775 to 1783. Grandfather Abraham travelled to Kentucky in 1782 with his friend Daniel Boone.

▲ Although he had little time to attend school, Abraham read books at every opportunity. Books were scarce on the Indiana frontier. He read the Bible, biographies and adventures.

Schooling

When enough frontier families moved to an area, they built a school. Children of all ages sat in one room. Abe Lincoln only attended school in the winter, when he was not needed to work on the farm. When he was older, he added up all the time he had spent in school and decided that it amounted to less than a year. Most children spent four or five years at school.

▼ School was held in a small cabin – just 8 m by 4 m. The teacher read the lessons out loud. Students repeated from memory what they learned.

▲ This is a page from Lincoln's maths book. It shows his work on a multiplication problem. Most children made their own books.

PUBLIC SALE OF
NEGROES
By RICHARD CLAGETT

THE WIDER WORLD

When young Abraham Lincoln worked in the fields, he was usually carrying a book. If people were chatting around him, he listened carefully to pick up a story, a joke or a bit of wisdom. By the time he was a teenager, he was giving speeches to townspeople about the American government.

When Lincoln was 19 years old, he was given a chance to see the wider world. A wealthy shop keeper in Indiana hired Lincoln to transport corn and flour to the port of New Orleans, Louisiana. Lincoln and a friend floated a flatboat down the Ohio River to the Mississippi River. The trip took three months. As the boat floated past the shores of Illinois, Tennessee, Arkansas and Mississippi, Lincoln saw how large the United States was. New Orleans was the first real city he had ever seen.

Lincoln and slavery
Lincoln saw the cruelty of slavery in New Orleans. At the docks a man had purchased twelve slaves in different parts of Kentucky and was taking them to work on a southern farm. Lincoln wrote about this to his friend, Mary Speed: "The (African Americans) were chained six and six together. . . like so many fish upon a trotline (fishing line). In this condition they were being separated forever from the scene of their childhood, their friends, their fathers and mothers, and brothers and sisters, and many of them from their wives and children."

▼ In 1828, New Orleans was a big city. Southern **plantation** owners sent bales of cotton to New Orleans to be shipped to northern factories and to European countries. **Slaves** were shipped there to be bought by plantation owners.

8

◀ Since the 1600s, some Americans owned **slaves** from Africa. Since 1808, slave trading with other countries was against the law, but it continued. Here, a slave brought from Africa **illegally** is being checked for diseases.

Still learning

When Abe Lincoln was 22 years old, he settled in New Salem, Illinois. He started working in a general store. The citizens of the town enjoyed chatting with this tall, thin stranger with shaggy black hair and a warm smile. They knew he read a lot of books. They enjoyed coming to him for a friendly chat or to ask his advice.

Although other people respected him, Lincoln felt badly about his lack of education. At the age of 23, he asked the village schoolmaster to teach him. Each evening after work, he studied literature, science, history and mathematics.

▲ This print was made by Currier and Ives in 1870. It shows steamboats and a flatboat on the Mississippi River.

▶ Slaves were sold at **auctions** as if they were farm animals. This book illustration, called 'Live Stock', shows a slave and his owner at an auction in Virginia in 1830. At that time, there were almost 13 million Americans. There were two million slaves, and more than 300,000 Native Americans.

◀ Abe and his friend brought farm products into New Orleans on an 18-metre-long flatboat made of poplar logs. He earned $24 for the journey. One night, just outside New Orleans, river pirates boarded the boat. Abe managed to throw the pirates overboard.

SERVING THE PEOPLE

Abraham Lincoln loved to study government and the law. He loved trying to help people and to make Illinois a better place to live and do business. In 1832, at the age of 23, he decided he wanted to be elected to the Illinois state legislature, a group of lawmakers.

Lincoln travelled to nearby communities to introduce himself. In one speech, he said, "Fellow Citizens: I am **humble** Abraham Lincoln. My politics are short and sweet. I am in favour of a national bank. I am in favour of the internal improvement system. If elected, I shall be thankful; if not, it will be all the same."

Lincoln lost his first **election,** probably because not enough people knew him. He spent the next few years working as a surveyor, planning roads and housing. He also worked as a postmaster, running a post office and delivering mail. Both these jobs took him across the state. He got to know many voters along the way.

Early elections and studying law

In 1834, Lincoln ran again for state **legislature**. In that year, he won his first election. He was a popular lawmaker. He was reelected to the Illinois legislature in 1836, 1838 and 1840.

In 1836, at the age of 27, Lincoln studied law books and took an exam to become a lawyer. The next year, he moved to Springfield, Illinois, the new state **capital**. The legislature met for a few months each year. The rest of the year, Lincoln helped people with their **legal** problems.

▲ Texas was once part of Mexico. In April 1836, Texans defeated the army of the Mexican General Antonio López de Santa Anna. Texas became an independent country. This illustration, painted by William Hudle in 1889, shows Santa Anna's **surrender**.

Around the country
1836 Arkansas becomes a state
1837 Michigan becomes a state
1840 US population is 17,069,000
1841 President William Henry Harrison dies after one month in office. John Tyler becomes president.

Lincoln marries
Abe Lincoln met Mary Todd in 1839. Mary's family did not approve of Abe. They doubted that he could support her in the wealthy style she was used to. Despite these objections, the couple married on 4 November 1842.

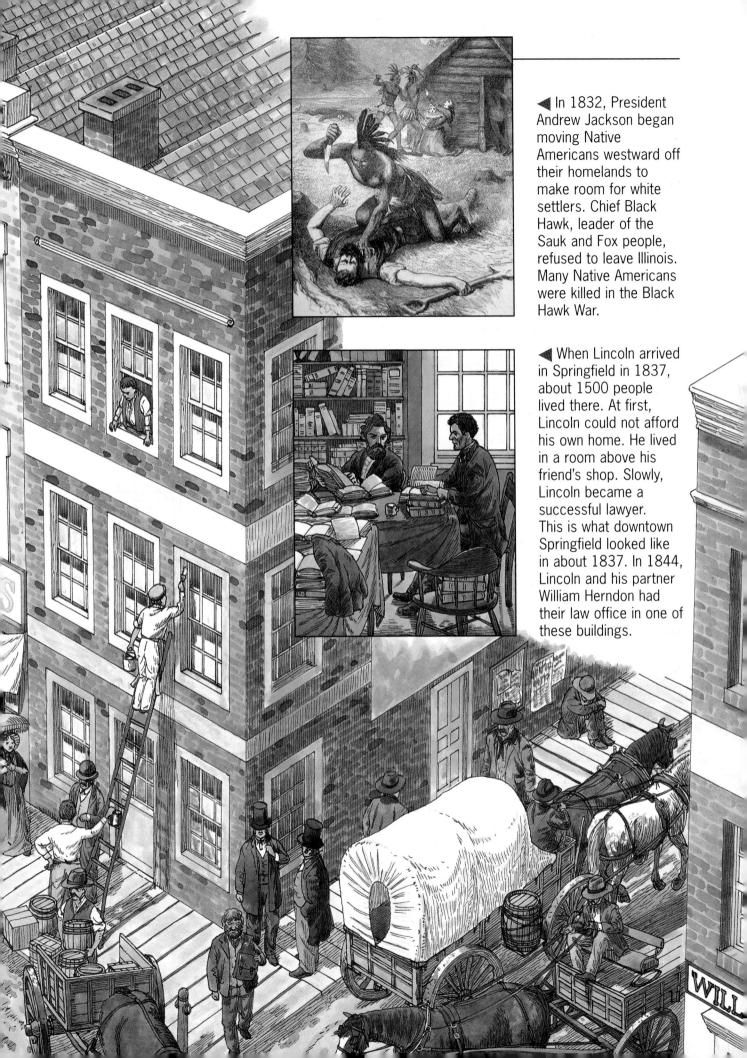

◀ In 1832, President Andrew Jackson began moving Native Americans westward off their homelands to make room for white settlers. Chief Black Hawk, leader of the Sauk and Fox people, refused to leave Illinois. Many Native Americans were killed in the Black Hawk War.

◀ When Lincoln arrived in Springfield in 1837, about 1500 people lived there. At first, Lincoln could not afford his own home. He lived in a room above his friend's shop. Slowly, Lincoln became a successful lawyer. This is what downtown Springfield looked like in about 1837. In 1844, Lincoln and his partner William Herndon had their law office in one of these buildings.

AMERICA'S NORTH AND SOUTH

Abe Lincoln in office
Lincoln was elected to the US **House of Representatives** in 1846. He and his family lived in Washington, DC, during the two-year term. In this period, the US gained Oregon Country (Oregon, Washington, Idaho) and bought California, Nevada, Utah and parts of Arizona, New Mexico, Colorado and Wyoming from Mexico. Abe did not run for a second term in the House of Representatives.

By 1853, the United States proudly owned all the land that would become the 48 states. Railways transported people farther and faster than ever. Telegraph wires carried news from city to city. America seemed more united. Actually, it was about to fall apart.

Most Americans lived east of the Mississippi River. Some lived in the North near factories. Others lived in the South on farms. Lifestyles in the North and South were completely different.

Cities in the North

By 1850, there were more than 100 cities in America. They included New York, Chicago, Philadelphia and Pittsburgh. **Immigrants** from Europe were pouring into the cities. Many worked in factories making such products as cloth, glass and iron. There was no shortage of workers. Immigrants and poor people would work long hours for little money.

▲ Between 1845 and 1847, there was a potato **famine** in Ireland. When the potato crops failed to grow, Irish farmers had little food to eat and little money. Here, officials are making farmers leave their home for failing to pay the rent. Many Irish moved to America to work in factories and build railways.

◄► This immigrant family from Ireland has no money to buy land in America. They settled in a small, stuffy room that is poorly heated. The father works 14-hour days in a cloth factory. The mother sews, cooks and washes for the family. When the children reach age 12, they will leave school to find work. Despite the hardships, they have a roof over their heads and friendly neighbours.

◀ This painting by an unknown artist shows a southern plantation. The plantation owner lives in a large house. Slaves live in a row of small cabins near the fields. Their small houses are used only for sleeping and eating. The adults and children aged six or more spend all day at work in the fields.

◀ This slave family knows nothing about city life in the North. They will only travel if their owner sells them or hires them out to another plantation. There are laws against teaching slaves to read or write. Slave-owners provide some food, but slaves must grow most of their food in their own small gardens.

The North–South divide

In the South, the government leaders owned large farms called **plantations**. They grew tobacco, cotton and sugar, which they sold to traders at markets. They used **slaves** to plant and pick their crops. In the North, most government leaders were involved with factories and businesses. They could manage without slaves. So, many Northerners were willing to support **abolitionists**, who wanted to make slavery **illegal** throughout America. Although most Southerners did not own plantations or slaves, the leaders in the southern states were against this.

THE GREAT DEBATE

"A house divided against itself cannot stand. I believe this government cannot endure, permanently half-slave and half-free. It will become all one thing or the other." Abraham Lincoln spoke these words on 16 June 1858, as he campaigned to become a US senator. He felt the country splitting over slavery.

America's arguments over **slavery** grew more bitter. The **federal** government was carving out **territories** in the West, such as Kansas and Nebraska. When enough people moved to a territory, it could become a state. Should the new territories allow slavery? Southerners said yes. Northerners said no – they wanted all new territories and states to make slavery **illegal.** Lincoln agreed with the Northerners.

Lincoln wanted the federal government to outlaw slavery in new territories. In 1854, he ran for the US **Senate**. He lost that **election**. In 1858, he ran again.

▶ In the Illinois election for US senator, Abraham Lincoln and Stephen Douglas held seven **debates** between 21 August and 15 October 1858. They were festive events, with brass bands and cannon fire. Only men could vote in the election. African Americans and Native Americans were not allowed to vote.

▶ This is Dred Scott and his wife. Dred Scott was a slave in Missouri. In 1834, his owner moved with him to Illinois and later Wisconsin territories, which did not allow slavery. In 1838, the owner and Scott moved back to Missouri. Scott believed he should be a free citizen after living in a free territory. In 1857, the **Supreme Court** decided that Scott was still the property of the owner.

The Lincoln–Douglas debates

In the 1858 Illinois state election for the US Senate, Lincoln's opponent was Illinois Senator Stephen Douglas. He was running for re-election. Douglas thought the citizens of each state or territory should be allowed to vote on slavery. Lincoln did not want to give the citizens a choice. He thought that slavery was wrong.

The two men held debates in seven Illinois cities. In a debate, opponents face each other and present their opinions. Thousands of people came to the debates. Newspapers reported them across the country. People everywhere paid attention to the words of Abraham Lincoln. Yet, he lost the Illinois election.

◀ In addition to their opinions, Lincoln (shown here on the right) and Douglas (in the centre) were different in other ways. Douglas was just over 1.5 m tall. Lincoln was over 1.8 m tall. Douglas had a deep confident voice. Lincoln had a high voice and a 'backwoods (country) accent'. He said 'git' for 'get' and 'thar' for 'there', Lincoln had a great sense of humour.

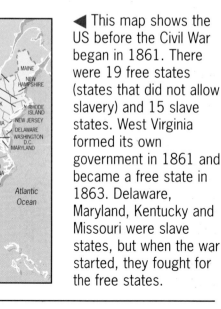

◀ This map shows the US before the Civil War began in 1861. There were 19 free states (states that did not allow slavery) and 15 slave states. West Virginia formed its own government in 1861 and became a free state in 1863. Delaware, Maryland, Kentucky and Missouri were slave states, but when the war started, they fought for the free states.

THE UNDERGROUND RAILROAD

"My Dear Mrs. Post: Please shelter this Sister from the house of bondage till five o'clock this afternoon – She will then be sent on to the land of freedom." Yours truly, Fred K (Frederick Douglass).

▼ **Abolitionists** hung this sign in Boston in 1851. It warned about slave-catchers who captured free African Americans and sent them south to be slaves.

The author of that note, Frederick Douglass, was once a **slave**. He ran away from his owner and eventually lived free in Rochester, New York. He and his wife Anne made their home a station on the Underground Railroad. They helped slaves escape to freedom.

A secret escape route

The Underground Railroad was not a railroad, or railway. It was a secret route of safe hiding places for runaway slaves. The route led from southern slave states to northern free states or to Canada. Many black and white people helped the slaves. Some of them let slaves hide in their homes, barns and wagons. They were called stationmasters. Other people guided the slaves from one hiding place to another. They were called conductors.

Slave-catchers

In 1850, there were more than three million slaves. Many tried to run away from their owners or masters, but most did not make it. Slave-catchers hunted and caught runaway slaves before they reached freedom. Slave-catchers often received large rewards for returning slaves to their masters. Slaves were severely punished for escaping, though they were not put to death. They were much too valuable to their owners.

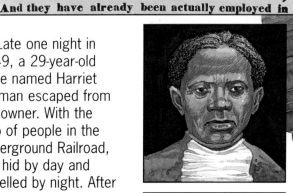

CAUTION!!

COLORED PEOPLE

OF BOSTON, ONE & ALL,

You are hereby respectfully CAUTIONED and advised, to avoid conversing with the

Watchmen and Police Officers of Boston,

For since the recent ORDER OF THE MAYOR & ALDERMEN, they are empowered to act as

KIDNAPPERS

AND

Slave Catchers,

And they have already been actually employed in

▶ Late one night in 1849, a 29-year-old slave named Harriet Tubman escaped from her owner. With the help of people in the Underground Railroad, she hid by day and travelled by night. After reaching freedom in Pennsylvania, Tubman became a 'conductor'.

Tubman returned south 19 times in 10 years. She led 300 slaves to the North. Slave-owners offered a $12,000 reward for her capture, but she was never caught.

In America's West
1843 the first large group of settlers head out from the town of Independence, Missouri, on the Oregon Trail
1848 gold is found in California and the Gold Rush begins
1860 Pony Express riders begin carrying mail to the West from St Joseph, Missouri

◄ Slave-catchers searched everywhere for runaway slaves. Clever conductors arranged hiding places in hay lofts, false sections of railroad carriages and below deck on ships. Some conductors acted as if they were owners travelling north with their slaves.

Free states
Slave states

CANADA

Great Lakes

Montreal

Collingwood
Niagara
Falls
Detroit
Chicago
Sandusky
Fountain City

Boston

New York City

Atlantic
Ocean

Portsmouth

Cairo

New Bern

0   125 miles
0   200 kilometres

Underground
Railroad Routes

▲ There were many secret routes on the Underground Railroad. They led from the slave states in the South to the free states and Canada. People in both the South and the North provided hiding places called stations. Some of these were shared by three different routes.

PRESIDENT LINCOLN'S CRISIS

In 1844, Abraham and Mary Lincoln were the proud owners of a house in Springfield, Illinois. That same year their first son, Robert, was born. Over the years, they had three more sons, and the Lincolns added more rooms to their house.

▼ This cutaway of the Lincolns' house in Springfield shows
• the downstairs sitting room, where the family relaxed with guests
• the guest bedroom upstairs
• the porch and balcony
• the wooden frame and brick chimneys.

▲ The Lincoln family owned this house from 1844 to 1887. It still stands at the corner of 8th and Jackson Streets in Springfield.

◄ Before becoming president, Lincoln was a successful lawyer.

► In this copy of a photograph, President Lincoln shows a book to his son Thomas (nicknamed Tad). Abe did not grow a beard until he was president. Only Tad and Robert outlived their father.

In 1860, leaders of the **Republican Party** asked Abe Lincoln to run for president of the United States. Men from three other parties ran against him: Northern **Democrats**, Southern Democrats and the Constitutional Union.

Many people in the North thought Lincoln would be a good president. He did not insist on ending slavery in the South, but he would not let it spread to the new **territories**. **Plantation** owners in the South were terrified of him. They were sure he would end slavery, ruin their plantations and make them poor.

Enormous responsibility

Abe Lincoln won the **election** in November 1860. He and his family left their Springfield house and moved to the White House in Washington, DC.

Lincoln knew the southern states were angry. He faced a serious and difficult job. As outgoing President James Buchanan was leaving the White House, he told Lincoln, "If you are as happy on entering this house as I am on leaving it, you are the happiest man on Earth."

The nation splits

The southern states took matters into their own hands. One month after Lincoln's election, South Carolina seceded, or left, the nation. Six more states followed: Mississippi, Florida, Alabama, Georgia, Louisiana and Texas. The seven states formed a new nation, the **Confederate** States of America. They elected Jefferson Davis of Mississippi to be their president.

◄ Lincoln's **inauguration** was held on 4 March 1861. Thirty thousand people came to hear his speech at the Capitol building. He spoke of the importance of keeping the states united.

WAR BETWEEN THE STATES

By the time Lincoln moved into the White House in March 1861, the United States government had an enemy. It was the Confederate States of America. The Confederate capital was Montgomery, Alabama. On 29 May 1861, the capital was moved to Richmond, Virginia, just 160 km from Washington, DC.

Many people in the North and South thought this new nation could exist peacefully with the **Union**. They were wrong. **Confederate** leaders insisted that all United States offices and soldiers be moved out of the South. Lincoln refused.

Fort Sumter was a US **military** base in South Carolina. Confederates insisted that this southern fort be turned over to them. In April 1861, Confederate cannons fired at the fort and continued for 30 hours. Finally, the Union surrendered the fort. The nation's worst nightmare had begun. A civil war, in which people of the same country fight each other, had started.

▶ Confederate soldiers bombarded Fort Sumter day and night.

▶ Abraham Lincoln (right) wanted to keep the states together. He believed slavery was wrong, but he was willing to allow it in the South for the sake of the nation. Jefferson Davis (far right), the Confederate president, was himself a slave-owner. He believed that each state should be able to decide if slavery were **legal.**

▶ Posters encouraged people to volunteer for the Union Army. By 1863, the Union required that all men between the ages of 18 and 45 serve in the army. This is called conscription. However, if a man paid $300 for a substitute to go in his place, he could avoid conscription. The Confederates had conscription since 1862.

THIRD IRISH REGIMENT

25 ABLE-BODIED MEN

CAPTAIN WILLIAMS

IRISH HERO

CORCORAN

THE GLORY of the other IRISH REGIMENTS

$150 Bounty

Captain WILLIAMS or. Lieut LEONARD!
No. 109 CAMBRIDGE STREET, BOSTON,

► Outraged over the attack on Fort Sumter, thousands of Northerners volunteered for the Union Army. They signed up for 90 days. No one expected the war to last longer than that. More than 2 million people served in the Union Army. At least 100,000 Union soldiers were under the age of 15. Many youngsters ran away from home to fight for their country. Some were sent by their parents.

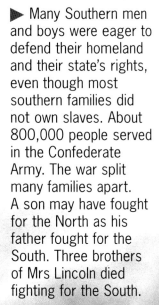

► Many Southern men and boys were eager to defend their homeland and their state's rights, even though most southern families did not own slaves. About 800,000 people served in the Confederate Army. The war split many families apart. A son may have fought for the North as his father fought for the South. Three brothers of Mrs Lincoln died fighting for the South.

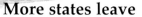

More states leave

By May 1861, four more states joined the Confederacy: Arkansas, Virginia, North Carolina and Tennessee. Now there were 11 Confederate states in the South and 23 Union states in the North. The leaders of states that bordered the North and South had difficulty choosing a side in the war.

The North had several advantages. It had 22 million people; the South had only 9 million. The North had almost all the factories to produce guns and other war supplies. The North had the most railways and control of the US Navy. But the Confederates had advantages, too. Many of the country's best military leaders lived in the South. They included Stonewall Jackson and Robert E. Lee.

THE BATTLES BEGIN

Washington, DC, the nation's capital, was just over the border from Confederate Virginia. To protect the capital, in July 1861 President Lincoln sent Union soldiers to fight the Confederates at a small creek called Bull Run. It turned out to be a bloody battle.

Northerners expected to win the battle quickly. But **Confederate** soldiers stood firm and fired accurately. Eventually, the **Union** soldiers turned and ran.

A congressman who watched the retreat reported: "The further they ran the more frightened they grew. To enable them better to run, they threw away their blankets, knapsacks, canteens and finally **muskets**." Confederate soldiers stopped to gather the Union equipment and added it to their stock. That day, 4878 soldiers were killed, wounded or went missing.

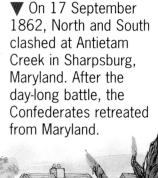

▼ On 17 September 1862, North and South clashed at Antietam Creek in Sharpsburg, Maryland. After the day-long battle, the Confederates retreated from Maryland.

Civil War Generals

Ulysses S. Grant – North Early in the war, he led Union troops to victory in Tennessee. In 1864, he became commander of all Union forces. In 1868, he was elected US president.

Robert E. Lee – South At first, he could not decide which side to fight for, but eventually he chose the South. In 1865, Lee became commander of all Confederate troops.

Stonewall Jackson – South Thomas Jackson got his nickname at Bull Run. He "stood like a stone wall", someone said. He died from war wounds in May 1863 at Chancellorsville.

William T. Sherman – North Sherman fought in the battles of Bull Run, Shiloh and Vicksburg. In 1864, he led an army that captured Atlanta and burned much of the city.

The Civil War was one of the first wars in history to be captured by cameras. Photographer Mathew Brady used a large, bulky camera and huge glass plates to take this photograph of President Lincoln with his generals on the field of Antietam.

This map shows Confederate and **Union** states in July 1861. Missouri, Kentucky, West Virginia and Maryland were slave states that stayed with the Union.

The worst day of the war

Several battles took place in and around Virginia. In September 1862, Southern General Robert E. Lee decided to try for a victory on Union land. He took his troops to Maryland, a slave state that stayed in the Union. He hoped that a great victory would make Britain and France recognize the Confederacy.

Lee might have succeeded, but luck was against him. At an abandoned Confederate campsite, a Union soldier found a scrap of paper wrapped around a packet of cigars. The paper was a message written by General Lee. It said he was taking his army to Antietam Creek in Maryland. The soldier passed the note to Union General George McClellan, who took his troops to meet Lee's at Antietam. The 17 September 1862 was the bloodiest day of the Civil War. Over 24,000 Union and Confederate soldiers died in the Battle of Antietam. But there was no outright winner.

BRAVERY AND SUFFERING

Most soldiers came from farms and small towns. Most had never left home before. Many were less than 18 years old. At first, the war seemed like an adventure. There were new friends, new uniforms and marching drills to learn. That spirit soon died as the youngsters found themselves aiming rifles at fellow Americans.

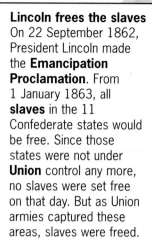

Lincoln frees the slaves
On 22 September 1862, President Lincoln made the **Emancipation Proclamation**. From 1 January 1863, all **slaves** in the 11 Confederate states would be free. Since those states were not under **Union** control any more, no slaves were set free on that day. But as Union armies captured these areas, slaves were freed.

When they were not in battle, soldiers practised marching and handling their rifles. A typical soldier carried 23 kg of belongings on his back. This usually included a rifle, tent, blanket, tin plate, cup, shaving brush, razor and comb.

Civil War soldiers suffered in several ways. Many were homesick, hungry and lacking soap and clean water to wash themselves. Disease killed more soldiers than bullets did – spoiled food, foul water, flies and mosquitoes brought typhoid, dysentery and malaria. Some medicine was available, but most doctors used guesswork to treat the soldiers.

▶ At each major battle, wounded soldiers had to make their way to a field hospital located 1500 m to 2000 m behind the action. Lucky ones were carried by friends or put in a wagon to bounce along a bumpy road. The hospital might have been a church, barn or farmer's front yard. Hundreds of men with every possible injury lay waiting for help. Only one or two doctors were available.

▶ This photograph in a gilt frame is of a **Confederate** soldier named Treasvant Childers. He was 27 years old when he joined the army. He fought in four battles and survived. After the war he became a farmer in Arkansas. He died in 1910. His older brothers, William and Thomas, were not so lucky. Both died during the Civil War while fighting in Virginia.

VICTORY
OR
DEATH

24

▲ This photo shows Confederate soldiers in battle.

Women step in

Not until British nurse Florence Nightingale helped in the Crimean War, 1854–1856, did women visit a hospital. In the US Civil War, women were desperately needed. Over 3,000 women stepped into field hospitals to take care of the suffering soldiers. Mostly, they wrapped bandages on wounds.

With men fighting in the armies, women stepped into jobs outside their homes. They ploughed the fields. They worked in the factories. In one Massachusetts clothing factory, 500 women made 1000 **Union** Army shirts each day.

◀ Doctors used tools such as these in the field hospitals. When a bullet struck a bone, doctors often had to cut off an arm or leg. Most doctors did not know that germs cause diseases. Washing hands and wearing gloves for surgery did not seem important. Some doctors took soiled bandages off one soldier and put them on another to dress battle wounds.

▲ A nurse tends a wounded soldier.

▲ A Civil War doctor's medicine chest.

▲ A surgeon's case of operating tools.

THE UNION'S VICTORY PLAN

The Union had a plan to choke off money, goods and supplies of food and medicine to the South. If the South could not ship cotton to Europe, it would have no cash. If European ships could not deliver supplies and weapons to the South, it could not survive.

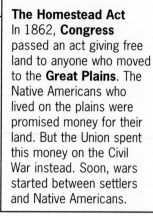

The Homestead Act
In 1862, **Congress** passed an act giving free land to anyone who moved to the **Great Plains**. The Native Americans who lived on the plains were promised money for their land. But the Union spent this money on the Civil War instead. Soon, wars started between settlers and Native Americans.

Before the war, the South had depended on the North and Europe for most of its **manufactured** goods, such as clothing, furniture and medicines. When the war started, the North stopped shipping goods to the South. More than ever, the South needed European goods. Also, the South sold much of its cotton to Europe. To make the South suffer, **Union** warships set up a blockade around the southern coast. A blockade stops ships from coming or leaving enemy ports. Though this put many British textile workers out of work, they supported the Union because they were against slavery.

▼ To remove the Union blockade, the South sent out an iron-covered ship called the *Virginia*. Then the Union navy sent out its first iron-coated ship, the *Monitor*. These 'ironclads' were sturdier than ordinary wooden ships. The two ships battled for five hours on 9 March 1862. Neither ship was sunk.

▲ During the Civil War, women left their homes to work in weapons factories. This woman is making bullets and other explosives.

▲ Southern women had an especially hard life. In addition to bringing up their children and running the farms while their husbands were away fighting, they lived in constant fear of Union armies marching into their homes to demand food. Because of the blockades, food, candles and medicine were in short supply. Even paper was scarce. Women often wrote letters on used wallpaper and old newspapers.

▲ Big guns like this one were used to bombard Vicksburg. "People do nothing but eat what they can get, sleep when they can, and dodge the shells", one citizen reported.

Splitting the South

The Union also wanted to take control of the Mississippi River. This would block the South's main transportation route. "Vicksburg is the key", announced President Lincoln. "The war cannot be brought to a close until the key is in our pocket." Vicksburg, Mississippi, was a key **Confederate** city guarding the river.

In May 1863, General Grant began around-the-clock attacks on Vicksburg. Finally, on 4 July, the Confederates gave up the city. The North took control of the river and the South was split in two. Texas, Arkansas and Louisiana could no longer send troops across the river to the main Confederate armies.

▶ Vicksburg, Mississippi, was under attack for nearly two months. It was too dangerous for citizens to stay in their houses. Many dug shelters in the hillside.

27

THE BATTLE OF GETTYSBURG

Gettysburg, Pennsylvania, was a small, quiet town with a wheat field, a peach orchard, a cemetery and homes for its 2400 citizens. The people of Gettysburg did not want the war in their backyards. They had no choice. Confederate troops were heading their way.

General Lee was feeling desperate. The **Confederates** had won several battles in the South, but much of the South now lay in ruins. Lee headed his troops to Pennsylvania. The **Union** troops of General George Meade met the Confederates at Gettysburg on 1 July 1863. The two sides fired heavily at each other until nightfall, killing a total of 17,000 men. At the end of the first day, the Confederates claimed victory.

▶ Days after the Battle of Gettysburg, bodies still lie on the ground. Nearly every house and barn has been turned into a hospital. The smell of death is so strong that people hold rags over their noses. The photographer has come to record the scene of death and destruction.

▲ At Gettysburg, on 3 July, General Lee ordered General George Pickett to march his soldiers across a wide open wheat field toward Cemetery Hill. The decision was disastrous. Union soldiers fired their guns and cannons at the parade of soldiers.

Overall, the Confederates lost (killed, wounded or missing) 28,000 men at the Battle of Gettysburg. The Union claimed a major victory, but lost 23,000 men. This is a **lithograph** of the battle scene by Kurz and Allison. It was published around 1890.

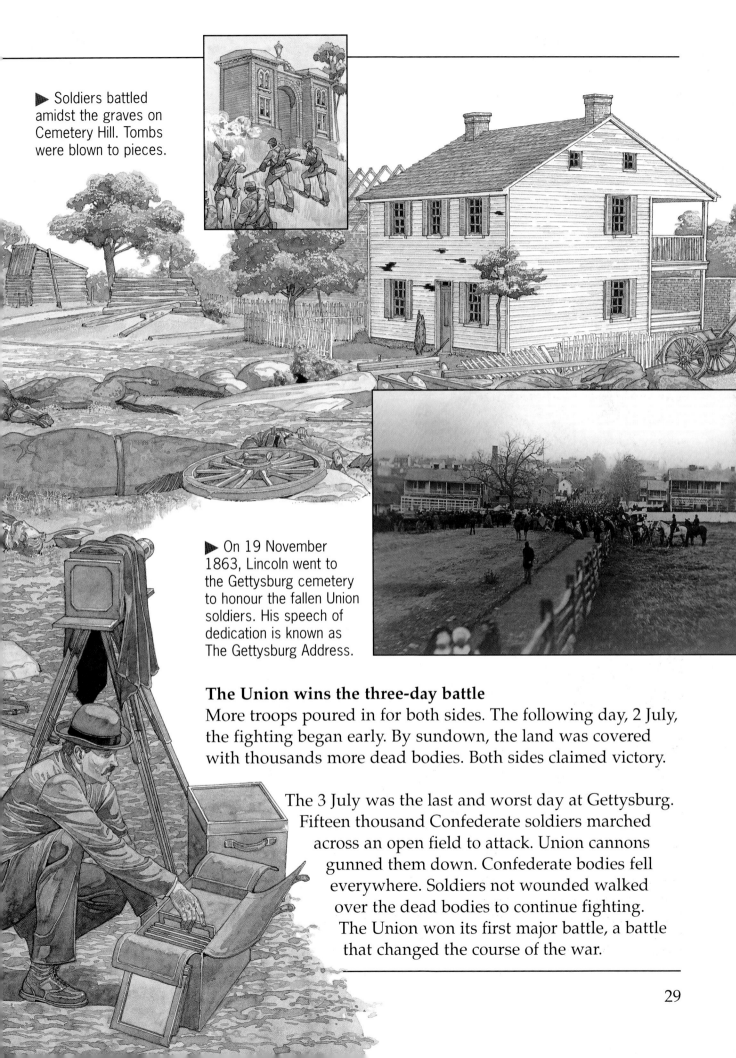

▶ Soldiers battled amidst the graves on Cemetery Hill. Tombs were blown to pieces.

▶ On 19 November 1863, Lincoln went to the Gettysburg cemetery to honour the fallen Union soldiers. His speech of dedication is known as The Gettysburg Address.

The Union wins the three-day battle

More troops poured in for both sides. The following day, 2 July, the fighting began early. By sundown, the land was covered with thousands more dead bodies. Both sides claimed victory.

The 3 July was the last and worst day at Gettysburg. Fifteen thousand Confederate soldiers marched across an open field to attack. Union cannons gunned them down. Confederate bodies fell everywhere. Soldiers not wounded walked over the dead bodies to continue fighting. The Union won its first major battle, a battle that changed the course of the war.

THE FIRST MODERN WAR

Since the beginning of time, a soldier's job has been to kill the enemy. As the world grew more modern, so did the soldier's weapons. Civil War soldiers were able to use the most powerful weapons to date. For better or worse, killing the enemy became faster and more efficient than ever before.

Some historians call the Civil War the "first modern war." New bullets, new guns and new cannons shot further and better than ever. There was the Spencer seven-shot rifle that fired seven times without reloading. A Gatling machine-gun fired 250 rounds a minute. However, the army generals did not know how best to use the new weapons. As in early wars, they lined up their soldiers to fire close to the enemy. This was murderous. All this made the Civil War the deadliest war yet.

Communications in the Civil War were also better than ever. Wherever troops moved, they set up **telegraph** poles and wires. Messages were put into code and instantly sent over telegraph wires from one army camp to another.

▶ This photograph from 1863 shows African American soldiers ready for battle. Men of the 54th Massachusetts Black Regiment won battle honours in South Carolina in July 1863.

▶ The North had many kilometres of railway tracks. Trains carried **Union** soldiers and weapons quickly and in great numbers from supply centres to the battlefields. This picture shows a Union supply station for weapons. With some success, **Confederate** soldiers sneaked into the stations and destroyed or stole Union weapons.

▲ Captured soldiers were taken to prison camps away from the battlefront. Hygiene in the camps was poor, and both the North and South treated their prisoners horribly. This **lithograph** shows a **Confederate** prison in Andersonville, Georgia. Over 12,000 men died there of disease and starvation.

▼ Some soldiers took to the air in hot-air balloons to spy on enemy camps. Others loaded and fired mortar guns (below right).

African Americans in the Civil War

At the beginning of the war, African American men were allowed to work only as cooks, drivers or scouts for the Union Army. In 1863, they were allowed to be soldiers, to fight for their freedom. Many from the North joined the Union Army and Navy. Southern **slaves** freed by Lincoln's **Emancipation Proclamation** in 1863 joined northern troops. In all, more than 200,000 African Americans fought for the Union. Another 200,000 worked as scouts, nurses, spies, cooks and labourers.

SHERMAN'S MARCH TO THE SEA

"War is cruelty. There is no use trying to reform it; the crueler it is, the sooner it will be over." Union Major General William T. Sherman summed up the Civil War that way. Sherman marched 60,000 men through Georgia, destroying everything useful in his path.

General Grant decided to threaten the South with a new kind of fighting called 'total war'. Northern soldiers would destroy anything that could help the South survive, especially farms, factories, railways and bridges. No place was safe.

Grant ordered General Sherman to march his troops from Tennessee to Georgia. To keep their load light, they carried no food. Instead, they sent soldiers called 'bummers' to demand food from the homes of Georgia citizens.

They captured Atlanta, Georgia, on 2 September 1864. They torched the city, leaving 80 hectares of houses, stores and buildings in charred ruins. From there, Sherman began his 'march to the sea' – the Atlantic Ocean – towards Savannah, Georgia. Along the way, soldiers stole mules, horses and 13,000 head of cattle.

▼ This photograph from 1865 shows the ruins of Charleston, South Carolina. Children sit among the rubble. The victorious **Union** Army soon sent fire fighters into the city to save as many burning buildings as they could.

Lincoln is reelected
In the November 1864 presidential **election**, Lincoln ran against his former army general, George B. McClellan. Americans had grown tired of the Civil War. Lincoln expected they would not vote for him again. But just before the election, Sherman captured Atlanta. Americans now trusted that Lincoln could end the war. They elected him president again.
    Lincoln proposed the 13th **Amendment** to outlaw slavery throughout America. It was **adopted** by **Congress** and accepted by the states in December 1865, after Lincoln's death.

▶ Atlanta burned to the ground while Sherman marched his soldiers towards Savannah, Georgia. As the Union took over Georgia towns, many **slaves** packed their possessions and followed Sherman's army towards freedom.

▶ As General Sherman and his troops marched through Georgia, they ripped up railway tracks and burned bridges to stop **Confederate** troop movements. They cut down **telegraph** wires, killed farm animals and set fire to crops.

▼ Atlanta citizens flee their homes, destroyed by General Sherman's troops. Most of the South's great cities – Richmond in Virginia, Charleston and Columbia in South Carolina and Jackson in Mississippi – also lie in ruins.

The end of the war

Though the North was winning battles, it was losing thousands of men. One account told of General Grant losing 60,000 dead and wounded in a single month. But Grant believed in victory at all costs. He knew the Union could replace both men and supplies. The South could replace neither any longer.

On 4 April 1865, the Union captured the Confederate **capital** at Richmond, Virginia. On 9 April, Lee **surrendered** the war. As the Confederates surrendered, Union troops began to cheer. Grant silenced them and said, "The war is over. The **rebels** are our countrymen again."

▼ Generals Grant and Lee met on 9 April 1865 to agree on the terms of surrender. They met in the home of Wilmer McClean in a small Virginia town called Appomattox Court House.

Civil War events
1861
April Confederates take Fort Sumter, South Carolina
July Confederates win at Bull Run, near the town of Manassas, Virginia
1862
March Battle of the *Virginia* (*Merrimack*) and the *Monitor* iron-clad ships
September Union win at Battle of Antietam near Sharpsburg, Maryland
Lincoln's **Emancipation Proclamation**
December Confederates win at Fredericksburg, Virginia
1863
May Confederates win at Chancellorsville, Virginia
July Union wins at Gettysburg, Pennsylvania. Union also wins at Vicksburg, Mississippi
1864
September Union captures Atlanta, Georgia
1865
April Union captures Petersburg and Richmond, Virginia
April Confederates surrender

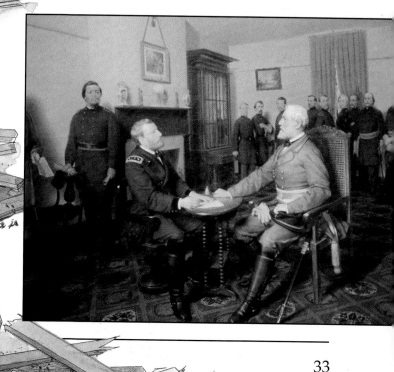

33

LINCOLN'S LAST DAYS

"With malice toward none, with charity for all, let us strive ... to bind up the nation's wounds, to care for him who shall have borne the battle, and for his widow, and his orphan; to do all which may achieve ... a just and a lasting peace."

Lincoln spoke these words at his second **inauguration** on 4 March 1865. He expressed hope that the war would end soon. In fact, it ended 36 days later.

Lincoln already had plans to reunite the states. He wanted 10 per cent of the people in each southern state to pledge loyalty to the nation. He wanted each new state government to outlaw slavery. Then voters could elect members to **Congress** and take part in the national government again.

Many members of Congress thought these requirements were too easy on the South. They wanted more than 50 per cent of the voters to pledge loyalty. They also wanted to take away the right to vote from anyone who fought for the **Confederates**. Lincoln was now faced with many **debates** with Congress. But he did not live to fight this battle.

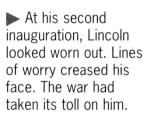

▶ At his second inauguration, Lincoln looked worn out. Lines of worry creased his face. The war had taken its toll on him.

"The President is dead!"

On the evening of 14 April, five days after the war ended, Mr and Mrs Lincoln went to Ford's Theatre for a rare evening of entertainment. As they watched a play, John Wilkes Booth entered the president's box and fired a pistol at him. Lincoln, badly wounded, was carried out of the theatre to a nearby house. Doctors could not save him. He died the next morning. Vice-president Andrew Johnson became president.

◀ ▶ After the war, many soldiers returned home to find their farms destroyed (left). Newly freed **slaves** (right) were penniless. These former slaves joined men from the **Union** army and worked on a **wharf** in Alexandria, Virginia.

► After the bullet hit the president, Lincoln's friend, Major Rathbone, tried to tackle Booth. Booth drew a knife and wounded the major's arm. Then Booth jumped over the railing and onto the stage. He broke his leg as he landed. Booth escaped from the theatre as the audience sat unaware that the president had been shot.

Booth's story
John Wilkes Booth was a respected actor of the time. He was in favour of slavery and sided with the Confederacy. He shot Lincoln because he blamed the president for the war. Several days after the assassination, US soldiers trapped Booth in a barn in Virginia, shot him and then set fire to the barn.

▲ Abraham Lincoln's funeral was held at the White House on 19 April. He was buried in Springfield, Illinois. His body was taken by train on the 2570-km-long journey. The trip took two weeks. This photograph shows the funeral train arriving at West Philadelphia Station on 22 April. As in other towns and cities along the way, Americans lined the tracks to bid their president farewell.

REBUILDING THE SOUTH

The Civil War was over. Nearly four million slaves were now free. However, most slaves had no homes. They also had no jobs, education or land. What would happen to them?

The freed **slaves** looked to the United States government for help. **Congress** created the Freedmen's Bureau. The bureau helped poor whites as well as African Americans in the South. Some Northerners moved south to start new businesses. Southerners called them 'carpetbaggers'. They said the Northerners arrived with a carpetbag – cheap suitcase – that they hoped to fill with money made in the South.

Many former slaves headed to the North to find jobs. Others stayed in the South. They helped rebuild the towns and railways. Some chose to work at their old jobs for their former owners. Many insisted, however, that their pay include enough money to build new cabins far from their old slave cabins.

Old laws, new rights

Many southern states had laws called Black Codes. These laws forbade African Americans to vote, own land or take jobs. Many whites in these states did not want Congress to give rights to former slaves. Nevertheless, in 1868, the 14th **Amendment** made African Americans citizens. In 1869, Congress proposed the 15th Amendment, which guaranteed African American males the right to vote. The amendment was passed in 1870.

▶ The Freedmen's Bureau is building this school in South Carolina. The bureau provided food, clothing, medicine and health care. It built 4000 schools and provided teachers to help former slaves read and write. By 1870, 250,000 students would attend such schools.

▲ This picture, called *The First Vote*, appeared in *Harpers Weekly* magazine on 16 November 1867. At this time, some southern states had returned to the **Union** and allowed African American men to vote. By the 1868 presidential **election**, most southern states had done so.

Impeaching the president

Many members of Congress wanted President Andrew Johnson to do more to help former slaves and to punish the people who fought for the Confederates.

In 1868, the **House of Representatives** tried to force Johnson out of office by impeaching him. To impeach means to bring an elected official to trial for wrongdoing. There was a trial before the **Senate**, but not enough senators believed Johnson had committed a crime. Johnson was not forced from office.

Alaska purchase
In 1867, the United States bought Alaska from Russia for $7.2 million. Many people thought this distant northern land was useless. But 30 years later, people found gold in Alaska. Then 101 years later, valuable oil was discovered.

No. 461 U.S. SENATE
To be taken up at MAIN ENTRANCE
U.S. SENATE

U.S. SENATE
Impeachment of the President
ADMIT THE BEARER
MARCH 13. 1868
Geo. T. Brown
Sergeant-at-Arms.
Philp & Solomons. Wash D.C.

▲ People could buy tickets such as this one to attend the impeachment trial.

PROBLEMS IN THE SOUTH

By 1868, there were new state governments in the South. Old leaders were out. The new leaders included African Americans and white people who supported them. They all wanted to change the old ways. However, the new leaders could not change the hateful feelings of many angry white Southerners.

Many white Southerners did not want African Americans to attend school, vote, become leaders or take well-paid jobs. It did not matter that a person showed talent, skills or manners. To white Southerners, African Americans were not equals. As a result, many African Americans started to feel inferior.

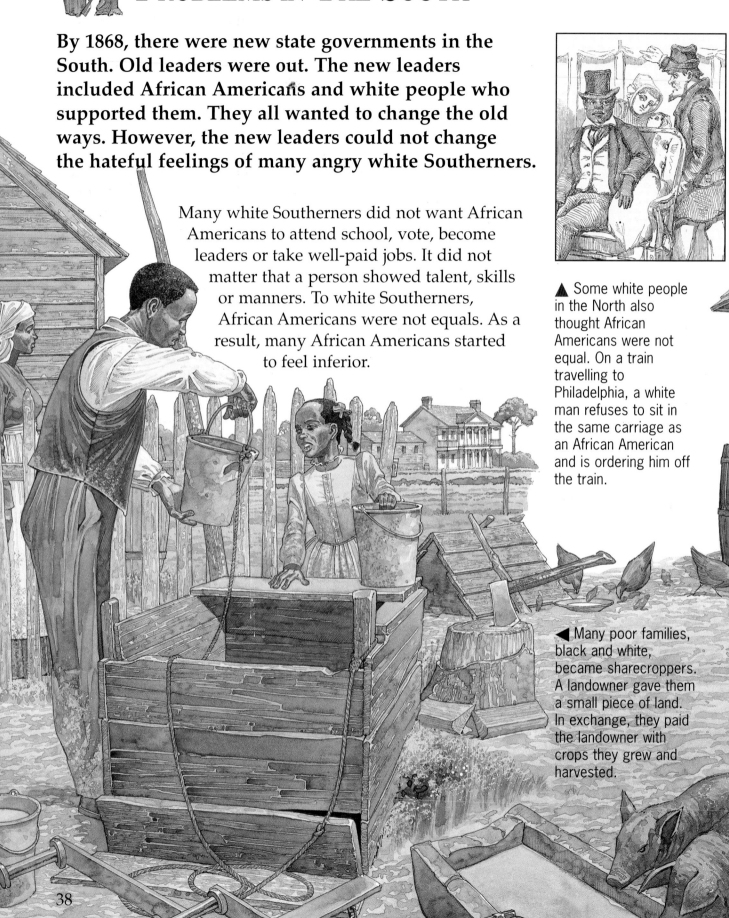

▲ Some white people in the North also thought African Americans were not equal. On a train travelling to Philadelphia, a white man refuses to sit in the same carriage as an African American and is ordering him off the train.

◀ Many poor families, black and white, became sharecroppers. A landowner gave them a small piece of land. In exchange, they paid the landowner with crops they grew and harvested.

▼ The Freedmen's Bureau had built schools for African Americans all over the South. Many white Southerners did not want African Americans to get an education. They burned down many new schools. This woodcut picture shows a Freedmen's school burning in Memphis, Tennessee, in 1866.

Anger in the South

Some white Southerners took matters in their own hands. They formed secret groups. The groups threatened African Americans and the white people who supported them.

One group called itself the Ku Klux Klan. Wearing white sheets and hoods to hide their identity and to look fearsome, they rode during the night carrying burning torches. The Klan burned homes, schools and churches. They often killed people.

◀ Because of new laws, African Americans were supposedly much better off. They were no longer **slaves**. They had the rights to go to school, vote and become elected leaders. Still, life was not good for African Americans. Most were given low-paid jobs, such as working on **plantations**. Most could not afford to buy land. Their lives were often at risk.

Reconstruction dies out

The **Reconstruction** governments did many good things in the South. They built hospitals, roads, railways and schools. Still, too many Southerners did not accept African Americans as equals. In the late 1860s and early 1870s, former **Confederate** leaders took over the governments again. They threatened African Americans to make them stay away from voting places. It would be more than 100 years before African Americans began to gain true freedom and equality.

CONNECTING THE CONTINENT

Before 1860, there were no railways west of the Missouri River. Anyone travelling west of the river took a horse, mule or stagecoach over rugged mountains and scorching deserts. Thousands of Americans did just that, for there was gold in Colorado and Nevada.

Mining towns were springing up in the West. Storekeepers needed to bring in food, tools and clothing for the miners. Railway companies knew they could get rich by providing a railway to the West.

In 1863, two railway companies began to build tracks that ran from the Atlantic Coast to the Pacific Coast. The line was called a transcontinental railway. The Central Pacific company started laying tracks from Sacramento in California eastwards. The Union Pacific began in Omaha, Nebraska, and built westwards. Thousands of workers laid heavy metal rails across wooden ties and hammered them in with spikes. It took 250 rails and 2500 spikes to cover one kilometre.

▼ The Union Pacific Railroad (railway company) hired ex-**Confederate** soldiers, former **slaves** and Irish **immigrants** like these men. The Central Pacific Railroad sent ships to China and brought back 7000 Chinese workers.

▼ Stagecoaches still carried people and mail, especially to places beyond railway stops.

▼ From a **telegraph** office, people sent messages along wires to distant cities.

▼ In huge factories and mills, new steam-driven machines mixed paints and weaved cloth.

▼ This steam-driven machine, built in 1869, was used to break ground for farming.

The golden spike

On 10 May 1869, the two railway lines met at Promontory Point, Utah. A crowd gathered and brass bands played. A railway official raised a silver hammer and drove a gold spike into the last railway sleeper. As telegraphs sent the message around the country, cannons blasted in New York. In Philadelphia, the Liberty Bell rang. Chicago held a huge parade.

People could now travel from New York to California in 10 days. They changed trains in Chicago, Omaha, and Ogden or Promontory, Utah. It cost about $75 (about $750 today) to travel first class. Now the country was truly connected.

▼ Buffalo and trains could not survive together. A herd of buffalo could take hours to cross the tracks. This woodcut shows passengers of the Kansas–Pacific Railroad shooting buffalo. The railway tracks ran through the hunting grounds of Native Americans, who needed the buffalo for food and clothing.

◄ The golden spike was hammered into place by the directors of the two railway companies. Later, the spike was removed and put on show in a museum.

◄ To lay railway tracks across valleys, workers built bridges, like this one. The workers blasted tunnels through some mountains. They slept in tents that had to be moved as the work moved along. The Central Pacific Railroad got supplies from the eastern states. The supplies were sent on ships that sailed around the tip of South America.

Historical Map of America

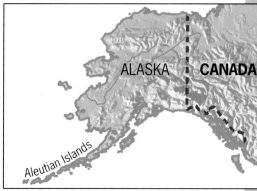

ALASKA   CANADA

Aleutian Islands

On the map

By 1869, the entire mainland of the United States was complete. In addition, Alaska became part of the nation in 1867. By 1869, there were 37 states. The rest of the land was divided into **territories**.

In the 1840s, thousands of pioneers left their homes in the East and followed westward trails to California and Oregon Country. Railways eventually connected the Atlantic and Pacific Coasts.

The US government and most of its citizens celebrated the country's growth. Unfortunately, Native Americans suffered greatly as they lost their homelands. This map also shows how the nation divided during the **Civil War** (1861–1865) and the sites of major battles.

Kauai

Oahu

Maui

Hawaii

HAWAIIAN ISLANDS

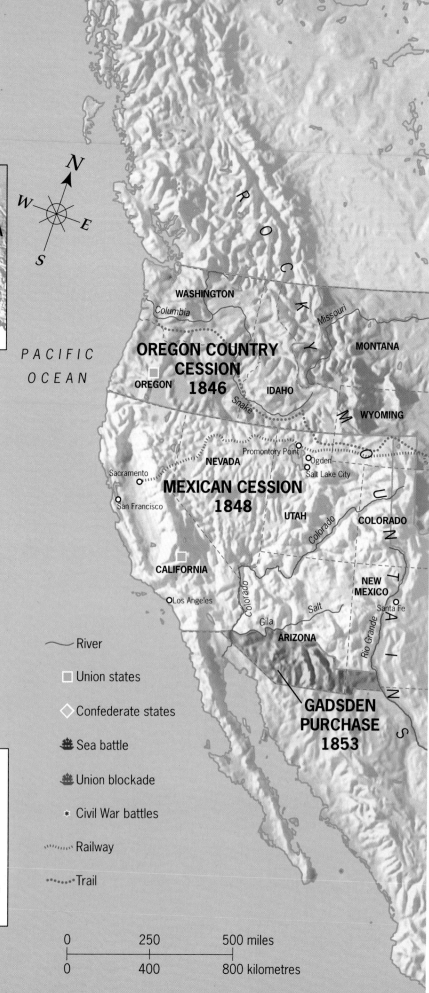

PACIFIC OCEAN

WASHINGTON
Columbia

OREGON COUNTRY CESSION 1846

OREGON

IDAHO

MONTANA

WYOMING

Promontory Point   Ogden
NEVADA   Salt Lake City

Sacramento

San Francisco

MEXICAN CESSION 1848

UTAH

Colorado

COLORADO

CALIFORNIA

Los Angeles

Colorado

Gila

Salt

Santa Fe

NEW MEXICO

Rio Grande

ARIZONA

GADSDEN PURCHASE 1853

Missouri

Snake

ROCKY MOUNTAINS

~~~ River

☐ Union states

◇ Confederate states

⚓ Sea battle

⚓ Union blockade

• Civil War battles

.... Railway

••••••• Trail

0	250	500 miles
0	400	800 kilometres

Hudson Bay

CANADA

RED RIVER CESSION
1818

NORTH DAKOTA

Lake Superior

SOUTH DAKOTA
LOUISIANA PURCHASE
1803

MINNESOTA

WISCONSIN

Lake Huron

MICHIGAN

Little Pigeon Creek

Lake Erie

Lake Champlain

VERMONT

MAINE

NEW HAMPSHIRE

NEW YORK

MASSACHUSETTS
Boston

RHODE ISLAND

CONNECTICUT

IOWA

Mississippi

Chicago

Lake Michigan

St. Joseph

Fountain City

OHIO

PENNSYLVANIA

Pittsburgh Gettysburg

NEW YORK CITY
Philadelphia

NEW JERSEY

DELAWARE

WASHINGTON D.C.

MARYLAND

St. Lawrence

NEBRASKA

INDIANA

ILLINOIS

ADDITION OF
1783

Omaha

Missouri

OREGON TRAIL

TRANSCONTINENTAL RAILROAD

Newport
Springfield

Ohio

Hogdenville

KENTUCKY

WEST VIRGINIA

Antietam Creek

Bull Run

Chancellorsville

Fredericksburg

Richmond

Appomattox

VIRGINIA

Petersburg

Monitor vs. Virginia,
March 1862

THE THIRTEEN
COLONIES
1776

Independence

KANSAS

MISSOURI

Fort Donelson

Fort Henry Nashville

TENNESSEE

NORTH CAROLINA

SOUTH CAROLINA

Charleston

Fort Sumter

INDIAN
TERRITORY

ARKANSAS

Memphis

Shiloh

Mississippi

Atlanta

Savannah

ATLANTIC OCEAN

TEXAS
ANNEXATION
1845

TEXAS

MISSISSIPPI

Vicksburg

ALABAMA

GEORGIA

LOUISIANA

FLORIDA CESSION 1819

New Orleans

The Alamo
(1836)

Rio Grande

FLORIDA

MEXICO

GULF OF MEXICO

CUBA

FAMOUS PEOPLE OF THE TIME

George Custer,
1839–1876, was the youngest general in the Union Army. In 1876, he led an attack against the Sioux and Cheyenne Native Americans at the Little Bighorn River, Montana. He was killed there.

Jefferson Davis,
1808–1889, was a Mississippi senator when his state left the Union. He became president of the Confederate States of America. After losing the Civil War, he was imprisoned for two years.

Stephen Douglas,
1813–1861, was an Illinois senator who believed that new territories and states had the right to allow or deny slavery. He won the 1858 senatorial election against Abraham Lincoln. He supported President Lincoln and the Union when the Civil War broke out.

Frederick Douglass,
1817–1895, escaped slavery and started an anti-slavery newspaper in Rochester, New York. During Reconstruction, he held various government offices.

Ulysses S. Grant,
1822–1885, was commander in chief of the Union army during part of the Civil War. From 1869 to 1877, he was the 18th US president.

William H. Harrison,
1773–1841, was governor of Indiana Territory and a congressman and senator from Ohio. In 1841, he served one month as the 9th US president. He died in office.

Sam Houston,
1793–1863, was a leader at the Battle of San Jacinto in 1836. This led to Texas's independence from Mexico. He became the first president of the Republic of Texas. When Texas joined the Union in 1845, he was a US senator, then Texas governor. He opposed Texas's secession and was removed from office in 1861.

Andrew Jackson,
1767–1845, was the 7th US president. He served from 1829 to 1837. He was the first president born in to a frontier family rather than a wealthy family. He started the Democratic Party.

Stonewall Jackson,
1824–1863, was a famous Confederate general. He fought in several Civil War battles.

Andrew Johnson,
1808–1875, the 17th US president, was impeached by the House of Representatives. Many people disapproved of his generosity to the South after the Civil War. The Senate voted to keep him in office.

IMPORTANT DATES AND EVENTS

THE UNITED STATES to 1850
1812–1814 War of 1812 is fought between US and Britain
1817 Mississippi becomes a state
1818 Illinois becomes a state
1819 Alabama becomes a state. US buys Florida from Spain
1821 Missouri joins nation as a slave state
1825 Erie Canal is opened
1830 The Indian Removal Act forces Native Americans off their land
1836 Texas wins independence from Mexico
1836 Arkansas becomes a state
1837 Michigan becomes a state
1843 pioneers go west on Oregon Trail
1844 first telegraph is sent
1845 Texas and Florida become states
1846 Iowa becomes a state
1848 Oregon becomes part of the US
1846–1848 US – Mexican War
1848 Wisconsin becomes a state
1848 Mexican Cession
1848 women meet in Seneca Falls to fight for equal rights
1848 California gold rush begins

THE UNITED STATES 1850 to 1869
1850 California becomes a state
1853 Gadsden Purchase
1857 Supreme Court decision in Dred Scott case
1858 Minnesota becomes a state
1859 Oregon becomes a state
1860 South Carolina secedes from (leaves) the Union
1860 Pony Express begins
1861 Kansas becomes a state
1861 ten more southern states secede
1861 Civil War begins
1862 Homestead Act
1863 Emancipation Proclamation
1863 West Virginia becomes a state
1864 Nevada becomes a state
1865 13th Amendment ends slavery
1865 Civil War ends
1867 Nebraska becomes a state
1867 US buys Alaska from Russia
1867 Reconstruction Acts are passed
1868 House of Representatives impeaches President Johnson; Senate acquits him
1868 14th Amendment guarantees citizenship rights
1869 the transcontinental railway is completed

Robert E. Lee, 1807–1870, was a famous Confederate general in the Civil War. In April 1865, he surrendered for the South. He became president of Washington College (now Washington and Lee University).

Abraham Lincoln, 1809–1865, was the 16th US president. In 1863, he moved to end slavery with the Emancipation Proclamation. During the Civil War, his main goal was to preserve the Union.

James Longstreet, 1821–1904, was a Confederate general. He fought in several battles during the Civil War. He disagreed with Lee's disastrous orders at Gettysburg, though he could not prevent the huge Confederate defeat.

George McClellan, 1826–1885, was a Union general in the Civil War. Lincoln criticized him for being too cautious and removed him from leadership. He ran against Lincoln in the 1864 presidential election and was defeated.

George Pickett, 1825–1875, was a Confederate general. He is best known for his unsuccessful attack against the Union Army at Gettysburg in 1836.

Antonio López de Santa Anna, 1794–1876, was a Mexican general and ruler. The Americans in Texas defeated him in 1836 and Texas became independent. He was also defeated by Americans in the Mexican War of 1846–1848.

William T. Sherman, 1820–1891, was a Union general in the Civil War. He led 60,000 soldiers from Tennessee to capture Atlanta, Georgia, and then marched to the sea, capturing Savannah, Georgia, and destroying the countryside along the way.

Harriet Beecher Stowe, 1811–1896, wrote an anti-slavery novel, *Uncle Tom's Cabin*, in 1852. People across the country became convinced of the evils of slavery.

Harriet Tubman, about 1820–1913, escaped from slavery in Maryland in 1849, and helped lead more than 300 slaves to freedom. During the Civil War, she worked for the Union army as a nurse and spy.

U.S. presidents to 1869

George Washington
    1789–1797
John Adams
    1797–1801
Thomas Jefferson
    1801–1809
James Madison
    1809–1817
James Monroe
    1817–1825
John Quincy Adams
    1825–1829
Andrew Jackson
    1829–1837
Martin Van Buren
    1837–1841
William Henry Harrison
    1841–1841
John Tyler
    1841–1845
James Knox Polk
    1845–1849
Zachary Taylor
    1849–1850
Millard Fillmore
    1850–1853
Franklin Pierce
    1853–1857
James Buchanan
    1857–1861
Abraham Lincoln
    1861–1865
Andrew Johnson
    1865–1869

ABRAHAM LINCOLN
1809 born on 12 February in Hodgenville, Kentucky
1816 moves with family to Little Pigeon Creek, Indiana
1828 travels to New Orleans
1830 moves to New Salem, Illinois
1832 joins military to fight Native Americans
1834 is elected to Illinois legislature
1837 becomes lawyer in Springfield, Illinois
1842 marries Mary Todd
1846 is elected to US House of Representatives
1858 debates with Stephen Douglas
1860 is elected US president
1861 Civil War begins
1863 announces Emancipation Proclamation
1863 gives Gettysburg address
1864 is re-elected president
1865 Civil War ends
1865 dies on 14 April

THE REST OF NORTH AND SOUTH AMERICA
1815 end of the war between Canadian and British forces against US troops
1821 Mexico, El Salvador and Costa Rica gain independence from Spain
1822 Brazil becomes independent from Portugal
1824 Peru gains independence from Spain
1829 slavery is outlawed in Mexico
1837 revolts in Upper and Lower Canada
1838–1840 Honduras, Nicaragua and Guatemala become independent from Spain
1841 The Act of Union joins Upper and Lower Canada into the Province of Canada
1867 Canada granted self-government by Britain

THE REST OF THE WORLD
1815 Battle of Waterloo between British and French – Napoleon Bonaparte defeated
1825 first passenger-carrying steam railway, in Britain
1839 photography first used
1839 Opium War between China and Britain
1842 China hands over Hong Kong to Britain
1845 potato famine in Ireland
1848 revolutions in Italy, France, Austria and Germany
1850 Australia granted self-government by Britain
1854 US forces Japan to open its ports to Western trade
1854–1856 Crimean War – France and Britain help Turkey against Russia
1859 Charles Darwin publishes his theory of evolution
1863 start of French empire in Indo-China

GLOSSARY

abolitionist person who is against slavery

adopt to accept an idea

amendment change in a document that becomes a law

auction sale where goods are sold to the person who offers the most money

capital city where the government of the state or country is situated

Confederate referring to the states that left the US during the Civil War

Congress branch of US government that makes laws

Constitutional relating to the laws of the state or national government

debate discussion between sides with different views

Democrat one of the two major US political parties that chooses candidates in the elections. As the slavery issue heated in 1860, the party split into Northern Democrats, who were against slavery in new territories, and

Southern Democrats who favoured it.

election process of choosing someone by voting

Emancipation Proclamation statement that freed slaves in Confederate states

engraving artwork made by cutting metal, wood or glass surface

famine serious lack of food

federal national

frontier land between a settled area and wilderness

Great Plains enormous flat areas of grassland between the Mississippi River and the Rocky Mountains.

House of Representatives branch of the US government that makes laws; it is part of Congress

humble not boastful or bragging

illegal against the law

immigrant someone who moves from another country

inauguration ceremony to put someone in office, such as the president of a country

legal allowed by law or referring to the law

legislature group of people with power to make laws

lithograph print made from a flat stone or metal plate

manufacture to make, usually with machines

military having to do with soldiers or war

musket gun used before rifles were invented

party organized group with similar beliefs about government

plantation large farm where often cotton and tobacco are grown

rebel someone who fights against the government or other authority

Reconstruction period following the Civil War when former slaves were given rights and new people in government tried to rebuild the South

Republican one of the two major US political parties that chooses candidates in the elections. It was formed in the mid-1850s by people who wanted to keep slavery out of the western territories. Lincoln was a Republican.

Senate branch of the US government that makes laws; part of Congress

slave person who is owned by another person and is usually made to work for that person

Supreme Court the highest court in the United States

surrender to give up or admit that you cannot win

telegraph device for sending messages over long distances – via codes of electric signals sent by wire

territory in the US, an area of land that is not yet a state

Union the United States of America

wharf platform where boats and ships can load and unload

MORE BOOKS TO READ

The World in the Time of Abraham Lincoln.
F. Macdonald, Belitha Press

A Soldier's Life. A. Robertshaw, Heinemann

Living Through History: Britain 1750-1900.
N.Kelly, R. Rees, J. Shuter, Heinemann.
Virginia plantation in 1859 in a secret diary.

PLACES TO VISIT

The American Museum in Britain
Claverton Manor
Bath BA2 7BD
Tel: 01225 460 503

Merseyside Maritime Museum
Albert Dock
Liverpool L3 4AQ
Tel: 0151 478 4499

Maritime Heritage Centre
Wapping Wharf
Gas Ferry Road
Bristol BS1 6TY
Tel: 0117 926 0680

INDEX

INDEX